UNDERSTANDING

DEATH

Why, Lord?

Why?

UNDERSTANDING

DEATH

Why, Lord?

Why?

Dr. Arlene Kearns Dowdy

†GLO†

God's Love in Operation (GLO) Publishing, LLC
920 Haddonfield Road #716
Cherry Hill, NJ 08002

UNDERSTANDING DEATH

GLO books may be ordered through booksellers or bulk orders may be fulfilled by contacting the author or:

GLO Publishing, http://www.glotutoringandpublishing.org

GLOInc2015@gmail.com

1-609-784-9698

All scripture references are taken from the Authorized King James Version, unless otherwise noted.

ISBN: 978-1-734-28212-2 Print Edition

REL012010   REL006080   SOC036000   SCI092000

Printed in the United States of America

GLO Publishing pub date: June 29, 2020

*Dedicated to the multitude of family members
who have lost loved ones to COVID-19*

Table of Contents

INTRODUCTION

A couple of months before the insurgence of the Coronavirus Disease 2019 in America, God led me to write and help people understand what happens at death. My racing thoughts were intrigued, first, by a word from my pastor. His request led me to an even more enlightening and in-depth study through the Scriptures. The discoveries of that study were clearer than all my numerous studies of death in the past. God, then, directed me to share my understanding with others. I got as far as an outline and a few notes but allowed other work to hinder the process. Then, COVID-19 happened.

As more and more people became sick, died or transitioned, either because of Coronavirus 2019, or because of other reasons, I knew why God told me to write and to share. Although my schedule has been thinly spread, I am determined to obey God and publish this work to help and encourage

His people with a greater understanding of death and transition.

I will preface this study and explanation with the fact that I am still learning. I endeavor always to become all that God has purposed for me, so although I am sharing with you what God has shared with me, I don't have all the answers. I can only give what I have been given.

We often find ourselves praying, "Lord, please, don't take her yet," or "Father, we need him a little while longer," or some sort of pleading for God to allow a loved one to remain on this earth.

When our loved ones do transition, are we left with feelings of grief? One needs only to observe the pain of a mother suffering the loss of her child; a wife grieving the loss of her beloved husband; a child mourning the loss of a parent or sibling. Yes. We feel grief.

Does God understand our grief? The prophet Isaiah wrote in a prophecy of the coming Christ, the Messiah, *"He is despised and rejected of men; a man of sorrows, and acquainted with grief . . . Surely he hath borne our griefs, and carried our sorrows"* (Isaiah 53:3-4).

Sometimes, though, we explain to our children, "God took them home to Heaven to live with Him." That explanation often opens up more confusion, questions and maybe even anger from the children. "Why did God take my daddy?" "Why did God take my mommy?" "Why would God be so mean to take my daddy? I need him! You need him!" The child, then, must live with confusion about the love of God and maybe even anger toward God throughout his life.

Are we correct in explaining a saint's transition as such? Does God truly take our loved ones from us?

One Sunday, I testified about how God worked miracles in my mother's life and restored her. I shared that I had asked God to restore her health. Then, if He wanted "to take her" after that, I would be more at peace and more understanding that sickness did not take her.

My pastor did not miss a single word. He, later, said so sadly, "Don't say that God 'took' anybody." He continued that topic for only about a minute or two, explaining that God is a loving God and does only good. He doesn't "take" anyone.

Yes, I know Job said, "*The LORD gave, and the LORD hath taken away; blessed be the name of the LORD*" (Job 1:21). Remember, though, that God had to correct Job about a lot of misunderstandings. Job expressed his feelings, and some of them were just that, his feelings. Remember also, the sufferings of Job did not come from God but from Satan. Job's declarations made him feel better and stronger and helped him endure a trying time, but in the end, God showed Job more perfectly who God really is. We, ourselves, make statements about God according to our knowledge, until we understand more perfectly.

"He doesn't 'take' anyone." These words of my pastor led me to yet another study of "Death" in the Scriptures. In my mind, I was searching the Truth in God's Word to verify what I've always believed. Instead, as God led me to one verse after another, passage after passage, He was taking me deeper into the knowledge of who HE really is, and God showed me where I have been "wrong" about death and transition. Then, just as Jesus told Peter, the Holy Spirit instructed me to strengthen the saints with the understanding He had given to me.

THE SHORTER VERSION

Rather than declaring what we have incorrectly stated for so long that God "took" our loved ones, we must begin to truthfully say what the Bible says for the Believer, that God "received" our loved ones in their desire and or need to move from their earthly bodies to their rest. On the other hand, they who have not died from their sins will have to experience that first death when "Death," overcomes them. That is devastatingly horrifying.

The first example I will use will be the first example that God showed me that day, that is of Stephen crying out to the Lord to receive his spirit. Let's take a look.

*"When they heard these things, they were cut to the heart, and they gnashed on him with their teeth. But he, being full of the Holy Ghost, looked up stedfastly into heaven, and saw the glory of God, **and Jesus standing on the right hand of God**, And said,*

> *Behold, I see the heavens opened, and the Son of man standing on the right hand of God. Then they cried out with a loud voice, and stopped their ears, and ran upon him with one accord, And cast him out of the city, and stoned him: and the witnesses laid down their clothes at a young man's feet, whose name was Saul. **And they stoned Stephen, calling upon God, and saying, Lord Jesus, receive my spirit.** And he kneeled down, and cried with a loud voice, Lord, lay not this sin to their charge. And **when he had said this, he fell asleep**"* (Acts 7:54-60).

He saw Jesus, not sitting on the right hand of the Father, as He is often described, but "standing." Why is Jesus, now, standing on the right hand of God? He is standing in honor of the faithfulness and martyrdom of Stephen and in preparation to receive His brother in the Gospel. What an honor! Jesus "stood" for Stephen. *"Precious in the sight of the Lord is the death of his saints"* (Psalm 116:15).

Jesus told the disciples in John 14:1-3,

> *"Let not your heart be troubled: ye believe in God, believe also in me. In my Father's house are many mansions: if it were not so, I would have told you. I go to prepare a place for you. And if I go and prepare a place for you, **I will come again, and***

receive you unto myself; *that where I am, there ye may be also."*

Again, the Lord speaks through Paul in 2 Corinthians 6:17-18 proclaiming,

> *"Wherefore come out from among them, and be ye separate, saith the Lord, and touch not the unclean thing;* ***and I will receive you,*** *And will be a Father unto you, and ye shall be my sons and daughters, saith the Lord Almighty."*

Another phrase, used first in the Old Testament but found also in the New Testament, that refers to what happens at death is "gave up the ghost" or *ekpneo* in the Greek, which is defined in Strong's Concordance as "to breathe out, breathe out one's life, breathe one's last, expire." "Gave up the ghost" indicates the person who embodied the "spirit" or "ghost" *gives* it up, NOT that God takes it from them.

And what is "the ghost"? The word "ghost" means a faint, shadowy semblance. What is a "semblance"? This word means "the slightest trace or appearance; a likeness, image or copy." The ghost is the spirit—that which God made us in the beginning.

"*And God said, Let us make man in our image after our likeness . . . So God created man in his own image, in the image of God created he him; male and female created he them*" (Genesis 1:26-27).

"*Then shall the dust return to the earth as it was: and the spirit shall return unto God who gave it*" (Ecclesiastes 12:7).

"*Then Abraham **gave up the ghost**, and died in a good old age, an old man, and full of years; and was gathered to his people*" (Genesis 25:8).

"*And these are the years of the life of Ishmael, an hundred and thirty and seven years: **and he gave up the ghost and died**; and was gathered unto his people*" (Genesis 25:17).

"*And Isaac **gave up the ghost, and died**, and was gathered unto his people, being old and full of days: and his sons Esau and Jacob buried him*" (Genesis 35:29).

"*Then fell she down straightway at his feet, and **yielded up the ghost**: and the young men came in, and found her dead, and, carrying her forth, buried her by her husband*" (Acts 5:10).

"*And immediately the angel of the Lord smote him, because he gave not God the glory: and he was eaten of worms, and **gave up the ghost**"* (Acts 12:23).

Finally, let us examine the words of our Savior, our example from God, who upon his death left us an example of both phrases. From the cross, Jesus cried out for the Father to receive His spirit, and Luke records that He "gave up the ghost."

*"And when Jesus had cried with a loud voice, he said, Father, **into thy hands I commend my spirit**: and having said thus, **he gave up the ghost**"* (Luke 23:46).

What is interesting about the patriarchs of the Old Testament is that, in many cases, they waited for someone or some event. They would wait until they had given their blessing to their offspring, especially to the eldest, but they never departed, until their work was done; right after their work was finished, their spirit let go of the body they inhabited, and their spirit departed.

How many of you have watched a loved one hold on, until he or she saw a certain someone or had a specific talk, or until some particular event happened?

According to the doctor, my uncle was at death's door, but he improved and went home. While he was at home, he had the chance to have some special, deep, meaningful discussions with loved ones and friends, wherein he counseled them in ways he never had before. Eventually, he went back to the hospital. There, he was not doing well, medically, at all. He kept sliding into unresponsiveness. Suddenly, he had a surge of energy and vitality. He sent the message to loved ones that if they wanted to see him before he went "home," they'd better come now. He specifically sent for certain loved ones. For the remainder of that day and into the evening, my uncle laughed, talked, loved and advised. Before day the next morning, my uncle "gave up the ghost."

One of my best friends lived at least ten hours from me, so traveling to each other was not easily accomplished. Throughout the years, we had spent many hours on the phone, when we could not get to one another face-to-face. We would have loved today's video chatting! She was sick unto death but was sending messages to me. I sent messages back, "Hold on. I'm coming." Before I could get there, she became unresponsive, had to be sedated and placed on a ventilator. I still sent messages, "Tell her that I'm coming." I got there, finally. Her sister and I spent the entire day in her ICU room talking to her, encouraging her, singing to her, praying and reciting Scriptures. At my coaching, she was breathing above the machine's assists. Then, I saw evidence that she really was suffering, even though she was responding and trying, in spite of her pain and suffering. At that point, I let her know it was okay and told her to rest, meaning for her to rest, until she was stronger. I thanked her for trying and hanging in there. We continued to talk, sing and pray. By the next morning, she had "given up the ghost."

Another young lady, a dear family friend, a sister, a wife, a mother began to suffer from a terminal illness, but she wanted to live. She recovered. Later, she began to suffer again. She wanted to live, and she recovered. Her sister told us that the next time around, she said she was tired, and she was ready to go. Although we sang, prayed and loved on her, she was so weak. It wasn't long before she "gave up the ghost."

My father was not well. He never wanted to be on a ventilator or any machine that would make him to live beyond natural means. He specifically requested this of my mother and me several years before he became sick. However, he consented to other concerned family members and the doctor to go on the ventilator for three days. Instead, the doctor kept him on the ventilator for seven days, despite my father's instructions. That was too long, and as a result, the surgeon had to perform a tracheotomy. He seemed to get better. The doctors said everything looked good, and he was improving, but my father let me know that he didn't feel different. He didn't feel better. He shrugged.

Eventually, he was transferred to the rehab part of the hospital, so he could regain strength in his muscles and learn to walk properly again. My father told some of us that he was not going back to that ICU again.

Although God had forewarned me that my father was leaving us, since he was in rehab, I thought I could now go on the ministry trip that I had delayed. I thought my father would depart from his home where he was longing to return. December 4, 2005, the last Sunday that my father was alive, I called his room thinking I would speak to a family member. Instead, to my wonderful surprise, he answered the phone! I was elated to be able to talk with him!

He transitioned three days later, Wednesday, December 7. I was told that one moment he was talking with the family. The next moment, he was in crisis, and the doctor ordered him back to ICU. The nurses came in working with IVs and preparing him for a quick move to ICU. Suddenly, he sat up quickly in his bed. Then, just as suddenly, his body fell back again, and my father had "given up the ghost." He wasn't going back to ICU.

There are so many examples of those who waited for someone or some event to happen before departing this world. These examples parallel the Word of God and the examples therein. What examples do you have? Let's speak what the Word of God speaks.

DEATH ANALYZED

What is death?

Maybe one reason for so much confusion and misunderstanding of death is that the word "death" is so multi-faceted: 1) To die or be separated away from your sins to live holy for God; 2) To die away from the body, or for the spirit to be separated from the body; and 3) To be separated from God eternally in hell.

Being separated from God because of sin is one death. We can die away from our sins to live in the abundant life that Christ offers and never have to die again. If you do not choose the abundant life in and through Christ, you will, of course, die the first death: the physical death-- the separation of your spirit from your body. But the serious tragedy is that you will die the spiritual death afterwards, the second death: in hell, you will be eternally separated from God.

As much as it pleases your fleshly mind to believe what pleases your flesh, there is no reincarnation. There is no dying in one form and returning in another. Those are mythical distractions to keep you from the Truth of the Gospel. As long as you believe that life continues to cycle in different forms, you will believe that there is no end, and you will not strive for perfect love and liberty in your lifetime. You believe you will have excuses and endless chances to "get it right." Those are all lies that Satan wants you to believe.

The literal definition of death *orthanatos* as defined by Strong's Concordance is "That separation of the soul from the body by which the life on earth is ended." The term "to die," according to Strong's Concordance is *apothnéskó* which means "to separate away from."

Historically, our ancestors believed that in death, the soul went to hell to suffer. Jesus solved that problem during His death and upon His resurrection. He took the sting from death and the power from the grave. *"Death is swallowed up in victory. O death, where is thy sting? O grave, where is thy victory?"* (1 Corinthians 15:54-55). Now, death has no more dominion over the child of God. When one dies

16

"separates away from" their flesh and sinful lifestyles to live in the spirit, they are the sons of God, and death cannot take them.

Death is man's enemy. Jesus Christ is our mediator and our Savior. He saved us from death. After we have died to sin, death has no more control over us.

"The last enemy that shall be destroyed is death" (1 Corinthians 15:26). Death is the enemy, and that enemy is not allowed to take the soul of even one of God's children. There is no more death for the redeemed and blood-washed Believer!

In April 2005, a few days after my mother buried her twin brother, we took a trip to Louisville, Kentucky for a church conference: my parents, one of my sisters and me. My parents ate something in the airport and were so sick at the hotel. I had picked up a few things to help them get better and was back and forth between my room and theirs.

Feeling better, my mother went downstairs with me to eat breakfast the next morning. Soon after returning to the room, she became sick again. My father, who was still sick and weak himself, called for me to come across the hall to check on my mother. She was so weak. I held her body up in one arm and with the other, I wiped her face with a cloth, praying.

Suddenly, her entire body became limp and lifeless; her arms dropped, dangling and hanging toward the floor! She was unresponsive! My father, watching from the other side of the room, was frozen in silence. Still holding my mother, I reached over her body with my other arm and called for paramedics. Thank God the phone was right there! Then, I began to speak to Death, because he was lurking. I didn't know, then, that he couldn't have her, but I did what I knew to do at the time. I firmly commanded, "Enough is enough! Death, you are a lying demon, and you cannot have her! You will NOT take my mother today! Leave her NOW in the name of Jesus!"

Suddenly, she began to move again and make sounds, but she wasn't talking. Still holding her, I called my sister to come over. She called Mother Curry. I don't remember who got there first, but the paramedics arrived quickly and prepared her for transport. That was an ordeal. Her pulse was so low, they could not detect one. In the ambulance, she passed out again, and they had to use a defibrillator to get her back. After her initial moments in ER, she seemed to be back to normal, and she was okay. All of the tests they ran for the next few days were all fine. They found nothing wrong. My dear father told me, later, that he thought my mother had just died right there in front of him.

The "shadows" of death are all around us, but death does not, cannot take God's children.

After you have separated yourself away from the things of this world, that is, you have died to sin to live the abundant life that Jesus gives; death has no more authority over you. You will depart this world when you "give up the ghost." Then, Jesus will be standing at the right hand of the Father to receive you, His child. When the saint is ready and knows the time is near, he makes ready for his departure, and the Lord receives him.

In accidents and otherwise spontaneous transitions, the spirit knows when it's leaving the body. Some decide to stay and suffer through, and others, for various reasons, know that their time is now; maybe they get a glimpse of Heaven, the angels, or maybe, like Stephen, even see Jesus welcoming them, and know that to be with the Lord is their ultimate goal.

My dears, even if you are not and cannot be with your loved ones when they depart, know that our Father, the Son, the Holy Spirit, and the angels are all around them, waiting to receive "their" loved one.

Let's recall how long men used to live. Adam was supposed to live forever in the Garden, communicating with God continually. However, Adam chose to sin. He chose to allow Eve to lead him into disobeying the clear and specific instructions that God had given to him. He chose separation. This separation or death, then, is a by-product of sin. Death is what happened as a result of Adam's sin, a result of the first man's disobedience. The serpent used the woman to cause Adam's downfall, which I might add is still happening to this day. When Adam made the choice to obey the serpent instead of obeying God, he was banished away from the presence of God. He died a tormenting, spiritual death that changed the course of the world and humankind.

Before the woman was ever created for Adam, Adam "had it all." Adam had all that man is still striving to obtain today: power, control, dominion and authority over the whole earth and, most importantly, friendship and daily, direct and loving communication with God—Adam had it all! And he let it all go with one choice, just one act. He disobeyed God, and it wasn't even necessary.

He allowed himself to be tricked. God had told him, *"for in the day that thou eatest thereof thou shalt surely die"* (Genesis 2:17). As a result, Adam was separated from His lifeline. His lifeline was the Garden, and above that, his lifeline was God. His disobedience, his sin separated him from God, his Creator. That is the first mention of death or dying in the Bible, not the separation of the spirit from the body, but man's separation from God.

Another "death," separation of the spirit from the body is the one mentioned in Psalm 116:15, *"Precious in the sight of the LORD is the death of his saints."* At the beginning of this psalm, in verse three, David expresses suffering, *"The sorrows of death compassed me, and the pains of hell gat hold upon me: I found trouble and sorrow."* Then, we experience the ups and downs of a suffering man throughout the psalm. Toward the end, he concedes with the consolation of the 15th verse, ending verse 16 with, *"thou hast loosed my bonds."* In this instance, David has suffered so much that he welcomes *maveth*, the Hebrew term for the existing condition of dying, "to sleep the sleep of death" or the separation of his soul from his body. Later in the New Testament, Paul expresses the same, welcoming death, the separation of his spirit to Heaven, as better than continuing his present life.

During the time of David, men were still living many years on the earth, so it is no surprise that David welcomed death over living a long life of suffering. Death, the last enemy, had not yet been conquered, though. Jesus would conquer Death with his own death generations later. Yet, that moment of separation was still said to be "precious" in God's sight. Remember, David was not only one of God's saints. He was known as a "friend" of God.

Have you ever been with anyone in their final moments? Have you watched as a loved one breathed his or her last breath? Even with sorrow in your heart, that moment remains with you. Whether you're holding his hand, resting your head on her chest, singing or praying, or holding another loved one, that moment is indeed a "precious" moment. We often want to be with our loved ones when they depart, certainly not wanting them to be alone in their last moments. Maybe Christ stands to salute us, as He did Stephen, when our work on earth is finished, while God sweetly welcomes His saints "Home."

Even before Jesus conquered death, hell and the grave, Jesus referred to the Believer's "death" as sleeping.

> *"Our friend Lazarus sleepeth; but I go, that I may awake him out of sleep. Then said his disciples, Lord, if he sleep, he shall do well. Howbeit Jesus spake of his death: but they thought that he had spoken of taking of rest in sleep. Then said Jesus unto them plainly, Lazarus is dead"* (John 11:11-14).

He used a term they could understand.

What Death is NOT

Ironically, a saint's departure should not be depressing and lead one down a spiral of pill-popping or any other addictive behaviors. We need not feel sad or sorrowful for the one who has gone home to glory. We must rejoice for and with the loved one who has passed from death to life; they have crossed over and no longer have to battle the everyday hustle or even the pain from a sickness.

However, if the sadness and sorrow is for ourselves, that is different, but that sorrow and grief must not lead to depression. The permanent absence of a loved one is physically and emotionally painful, and you will miss them. Sometimes, you wish the person could return just for a moment longer. You mourn, weep, and grieve, but only for a time. Sometimes our sorrow is not for ourselves but for the deceased family members left behind: the spouse, children, parents, siblings, etc.

In behalf of the saint, though, death is not sorrowful. Death is not foreboding for a saint.

One's departure is not something done to him or even breath taken from him. The separation of the spirit away from one's body happens when that child of God *gives up the ghost*.

Many people throughout the ages have taught that the weeping of Jesus when Lazarus died was because of what the Jew said, *"Oh, how he loved him"* (John 11:36). How often did the Jews have any correct understanding concerning Jesus Christ? There is a deeper reason for the weeping of Jesus that day, a reason so deep that Jesus "groaned" and was "troubled" (*tarasso* –a deep spiritual and emotional fear and dread) in His spirit. He was about to display a huge miracle! Jesus was about to show everyone a resurrection from the grave! What would be the deep fear and dread that would cause Jesus to groan about that? In fact, He had already declared to His disciples in verse 15 that He was "glad" He was not there, so they could see the glory of God. I seriously encourage the Bible scholar to carefully read each verse from the 11th chapter of John through the 13th chapter and truly follow Jesus Christ through the verses to understand. I don't want to distract further from the purpose of this current topic, but can you recall another time when Jesus was exceedingly sorrowful? How is that event connected to this one? Let me get back to the topic.

Death is not the "end" of life; death is only the end of life on earth on this side of Heaven. Death is not "the end." Death is only a separation, for life continues.

Let's look at the creation of God that He called "Man." Gen 2:7 explains, *"And the LORD God . . . breathed into his nostrils the breath of life; and man became a living soul,"* using the Hebrew term "chay," an adjective meaning "lively or alive."

So, now, this Man that the Godhead, "us," made or fashioned out of the earth has a concrete body to be a house or temple for the spiritual man He created after His own image. This earthly body can stand and walk upright, use his mouth to talk, using speech like them, has a more developed brain than the animals for more complex thinking, understanding, planning, choosing, and he can communicate with God! He also has the capacity to rule over the earth! He has arms, hands, and an extreme ability and capacity to create and implement great ideas! This Man has the image of God and HIS likeness. This Man, this earthy body, formed with the dust of the earth, is made alive with the *breathed* ("*naphach*" -- to breathe, blow, give up or lose life) *breath* ("*neshamah*" -- breath of God, spirit of man) of life from God's own life. GOD breathed some of HIMSELF into the body He had just created, and now, the body is alive, lively, activated with God's own spirit, life and likeness!

Death can in no wise come from God who is the very essence and Creator of Life. Thus, death is not a punishment from God. Death is not an angel from God. Death was never a part of God's plan, but it is a by-product and result of man's disobedience. Now, the body that was formed from the dust of the earth must return to the earth.

However, "*We shall not all sleep, but we shall all be changed, In a moment, in the twinkling of an eye*" (1 Corinthians 15:51-52).

What Happens at Death

"*Then shall the dust return to the earth as it was: and the spirit shall return unto God who gave it*" (Ecclesiastes 12:7).

The saints of God or Believers are they who have repented of, turned away from, their sins and are born again. Their lives are changed to walk no more in the sinful lifestyles and pleasures of the flesh, but they walk in the Spirit. Paul explains this in his book to the people of Colossae.

"For ye are dead, and your life is hid with Christ in God. . . Mortify therefore your members which are upon the earth; fornication, uncleanness, inordinate affection, evil concupiscence, and covetousness, which is idolatry: For which things' sake the wrath of God cometh on the children of disobedience: In the which ye also walked some time, when ye lived in them. But now ye also put off all these; anger, wrath, malice, blasphemy, filthy communication out of your mouth. Lie not one to another, seeing that ye have put off the old man with his deeds; And have put on the new man, which is renewed in knowledge after the image of him that created him" (Colossians 3:3-10).

Because he already has learned and has been walking in the spirit, when the Believer's spirit leaves his body, he never has to experience death's terror of being taken into darkness. Instead, the Bible indicates that when the spirit of the saint leaves his body, he sleeps or goes into his rest. Jesus stands at the right hand of the Father to

29

welcome them home. The Bible records Stephen's separation as peaceful, even in the midst of being treated violently, *"And when he had said this, he fell asleep."*

"But now is Christ risen from the dead, and become the firstfruits of them that slept" (1 Corinthians 15:20). When saints depart, they continue to follow Christ. The death and resurrection of Jesus made Him the example for us who would, one day, follow Him. Saints fall asleep to a much needed rest from their labor, until the day of Christ. When Jesus comes again, those who sleep in Christ, *"the dead in Christ,"* will be the first to rise. One of my late pastors used to always say, "Sleep on, now! But they can't crown you 'til I get there!" Hallelujah!

An old hymn was on my lips and in my heart as I awoke one morning. I had not heard this song in many years, so I found it and sang as I listened over and over. All I ever knew of the song was the chorus, but I learned that this song, written by R. H. Cornelius in 1916, has four verses. The passionate longing to see the Lord is evident in these lyrics.

Verse One:
*"As I journey through the land, singing as I go,
Pointing souls to Calvary, to the crimson flow,*

Many arrows pierce my soul from without, within;
But my Lord leads me on, through Him I must win.

Chorus:
Oh I want to see Him, Look upon His face.
There to sing forever of His saving grace;
On the streets of Glory, let me lift my voice;
Cares all past, home at last, ever to rejoice

Verse 2:
When in service for my Lord, dark may be the night,
But I'll cling more closely to Him, He will give me light;
Satan's snares may vex my soul, Turn my thoughts aside;
But my Lord goes ahead, leads whate'er betide.

Verse 3:
When in valleys low I look, toward the mountain height,
And behold my Savior there, leading in the fight,
With a tender hand outstretched, toward the valley low,
Guiding me, I can see, as I onward go.

Verse 4:
When before me billows rise, from the mighty deep,
Then my Lord directs my bark; he doth safely keep,
And He leads me gently on through this world below;
He's a real friend to me, Oh, I love Him so.

Chorus:

Oh I want to see Him, Look upon His face.
There to sing forever of His saving grace;
On the streets of Glory, let me lift my voice;
Cares all past, home at last, ever to rejoice

Sadly, though, for the non-believer, the sinner, the one who would not accept Jesus Christ as his personal Savior, the one who refused to repent of his sins and turn away from them to obey God, he experiences two deaths.

The first death: He does not get to experience Jesus standing at the right hand of God to honor him for a job well done. He does not have anyone to welcome him to a paradise he can call home. He does not have a mansion prepared by Jesus Christ, Himself, just waiting for his rest. Instead, the sinner must go into a dark grave of terror, awaiting judgment. His first death is when his spirit separates from his body. His breath or life is taken away. The spirit that remains for him is the wickedness of the god he followed and obeyed throughout his lifetime—Satan.

The second death for the sinner happens at the time of judgment: the eternal separation from God and all that is Love and Light, and he is condemned to hell for eternity. He is eternally separated from God, never again to see or feel the Light and Love of Christ.

> "*And the sea gave up the dead which were in it; and death and hell delivered up the dead which were in them: and they were judged every man according to their works. And death and hell were cast into the lake of fire. This is the second death. And whosoever was not found written in the book of life was cast into the lake of fire*" (Revelation 20:13 – 15).

THE SAINT'S ATTITUDE REGARDING DEATH

Should the separation of our loved ones be an extended time of anguish and pain? How does one break away from these feelings?

Certainly, for the loved ones left behind, there is naturally a season of sorrow, tears, and a time of grief and emotional pain that sometimes triggers physical pain and anguish, but this season should not be prolonged. Sadness and tears may be periodic, yes, but not grief. An extension of grief indicates a spirit of sorrow that needs to be cast out because *"where the Spirit of the Lord is, there is liberty"* (2 Corinthians 3:17). There is no bondage to sorrow or grief where the Spirit of the Lord is. *"And the spirit of the Lord shall rest upon him, the spirit of wisdom and understanding, the spirit of counsel and might, the spirit of knowledge and of the fear of the Lord"* (Isaiah 11:2).

Instead of grief, one must understand death; one must be counseled and be able to give counsel. The Spirit of the Lord gives knowledge and is mighty to pull down strongholds. *"But the Spirit of the Lord departed from Saul, and an evil spirit from the Lord troubled him"* (1 Samuel 16:14). It is not of the Lord's Spirit for one to be troubled with a spirit of grief, still trying to understand why the loved one had to depart. All spirits originated in Heaven, but Satan and a third of the angels were banished out of Heaven when Satan thought he could be equal to God. Even now, Satan cannot touch a child of God without God's permission. Know that Satan does not want anyone to be happy in Christ, so he finds every wicked way possible to trouble one's heart and mind.

So, what is our attitude for loved ones who sleep in Christ? Let's look to the aged women, to those who are full of the wisdom of God. When calmly and cautiously revealing to our mother that someone extremely dear to her had transitioned, to our amazement, she did not get upset. She simply responded, "He just beat me running." Another mother in her eighties was sharing with me after burying two sons, "Well, I guess you think about all the things that could happen, and you see yourself going through it

36

with strength. That's what I do, and when it happens, you're able to go through that in a way that just doesn't make sense, I guess." She also quoted Isaiah 53:4 when Isaiah prophesies about the promised Messiah, "*Surely he hath borne our griefs, and carried our sorrows.*" It helps to know that your loved one is at rest in a better place and with the Lord. You rejoice to know that they have made it, and their journey on earth is over. "*But I would not have you to be ignorant, brethren, concerning them which are asleep, that ye sorrow not, even as others which have no hope*" (1 Thessalonians 4:13).

So, if you find yourself unable to rise up from the loss of a loved one; if you find yourself unable to move on and live life; unable to love on and sincerely show appreciation to those around you, reach out to an intercessor, a prayer warrior who can help you out of bondage. If you don't know one, begin to pray now for your deliverance. We no longer have to have a human mediator to reach our Father God for us. We can boldly and confidently go to the Throne of Grace for ourselves. Begin to rejoice and praise with an attitude of gratitude for the time you had with the loved one; recognize the blessing God gave you that they were in your life at all and rejoice. Then, finally, release your loved one into the hands of

God; thereby, releasing yourself to love God, actively love others more, and most importantly, be used by God to demonstrate HIS glory.

Live in peace. We use the adage, "Rest in Peace (R.I.P.)" but is that what we really want for the loved one? Make sure your words and your actions represent your true feelings, and your feelings are in alignment with the Word of God. Don't let your feelings and emotions control your thoughts, words and actions. Instead, control your feelings and emotions by your thoughts, words and actions. Speak power, life, strength, courage and overcome.

Now, about your own death, should you fear death and dying? Should you dread the thought of leaving these temporary bodies and the wickedness on this earth? Should you despise the thought that maybe your work is done? Should you be sorrowful when it is, finally, your time and opportunity to see the "blessed face of Him who died for me [who] sacrificed His life for my liberty," as sung by Yolanda Adams? Should we be trying our best to remain on this earth when our time to leave this earth is come? Should we fight to stay with loved ones here on earth rather than to depart and be with God who IS Love?

Paul proclaimed,

"*For to me to live is Christ, and to die is gain. . . . For I am in a strait betwixt two, having a desire to depart, and to be with Christ; which is far better: Nevertheless to abide in the flesh is more needful for you*" (Philippians 1:21, 23-24).

Jesus said,

"*In my Father's house are many mansions: if it were not so, I would have told you. I go to prepare a place for you. And if I go and prepare a place for you, I will come again, and receive you unto myself; that where I am, there ye may be also*" (John 14:2-3).

"*These all died in faith, not having received the promises, but having seen them afar off, and were persuaded of them, and embraced them, and confessed that they were strangers and pilgrims on the earth . . .But now they desire a better country, that, an heavenly: wherefore God is not ashamed to be called their God: for he hath prepared for them a city*" (Hebrews 11:13, 16).

"*O death, where is thy sting? O grave, where is thy victory? The sting of death is sin; and the strength of sin is the law*" (1 Corinthians 15:55-56).

> *"For if we believe that Jesus died and rose again, even so them also which sleep in Jesus will God bring with him. For this we say unto you by the word of the Lord, that we which are alive and remain unto the coming of the Lord shall not prevent them which are asleep. For the Lord himself shall descend from heaven with a shout, with the voice of the archangel, and with the trump of God: and the dead in Christ shall rise first: Then we which are alive and remain shall be caught up together with them in the clouds, to meet the Lord in the air: and so shall we ever be with the Lord. Wherefore comfort one another with these words"* (1 Thessalonians 4:14-18).

For the saint of God, being with the Lord is far better.

However, the opposite is true if you have not repented of your sins. If you have not separated yourself away from a life of sin, you have every need to fear death, the separation of your soul from your flesh and, most importantly, the separation of your soul from God eternally. You have every right to fear the damnation that is yours and the sentence of everlasting fire that was never even prepared for you. This everlasting fire was prepared for the devil and his angels or demons. *"Then shall he say also unto them on the left hand,*

Depart from me, ye cursed, into everlasting fire, prepared for the devil and his angels" (Matthew 25:41). *"And he cried and said, Father Abraham, have mercy on me, and send Lazarus, that he may dip the tip of his finger in water, and cool my tongue; for I am tormented in this flame"* (Luke 16:24). Yes, sinner man and those who have gone out of fellowship with Christ, you have much of which to be fearful.

Should we prefer to live on earth?

Well, let's consider Lot's wife. *"But his wife looked back from behind him, and she became a pillar of salt"* (Genesis 19:26).

Angels came to deliver Lot and his family from a wicked and perverse land full of sodomites and misguided people. There could not be found even ten righteous people in the whole land. In the midst of that kind of terror, evil and sorrow, you would think that Lot and his wife would have rejoiced that angels had come to deliver them and would have quickly packed up and left the same day the angels came.

41

These people were so wicked that just because they saw two strange men go into Lot's house, they thought they had some kind of "right" to them. Because protecting guests in their home was of the utmost importance in their culture, Lot went so far as to even offer them his two virgin daughters, so they leave his guests alone. They wanted nothing to do with the daughters; they wanted the male guests, and they were going to beat Lot down and break down the door of his house to get to them! The angels, the male guests, pulled Lot into the house and immediately caused all the men to become blind. Suddenly, they were no longer so bold and strong. Instead, they were confused, weak and powerless to change their situation.

Regardless of this horrifying and dangerous incident, Lot and his wife still were not anxious to leave Sodom! They lingered, until the angels had to grab their hands to escort them out! That wasn't enough. The heart of Lot's wife, whether longing for the married daughters whose husbands refused to leave and did not want them to be destroyed or just longing for the place she called "home" no matter how wicked it was, was so attached to that "place" she was leaving that she turned around for one more view—that was one time too many. She immediately turned into a pillar of salt. I imagine Lot and his daughters probably wanted to stay there and scream, cry and grieve, but they were under instructions to leave quickly, and they just had to keep going.

There is definitely a serious reason why we are admonished to "Remember Lot's wife" (Luke 17:32). We get so attached to our things, activities, loved ones, friends, homes, special places, etc. that our minds are more focused on them than they are on God and our salvation. We can become so divided within our own minds and hearts, having a desire to please God but constantly looking away from him to earthly pleasures, and "*A double minded man is unstable in all his ways*" (James 1:8). We have to remember the intimate prayer of Jesus to His father, as He prayed for His disciples, "*They are not of the world, even as I am not of the world*" (John 17:16). This world is not our home. We have to be loosed of its affections and strongholds.

Isn't this world becoming a world much like Sodom, with its wickedness, killing, acceptance and promotion of homosexuality, immorality and other sins and abominations? Yet, you would rather live in this world than go to Heaven? When you feel that your time to depart is near, do you plead with God like Hezekiah for more time on the earth, or are you more like Moses?

When God informed Moses that he was about to depart, I never saw where Moses was sad, upset or where he questioned why he had to depart. In fact, reading Moses' conversations with God as He led the Israelites makes me laugh sometimes. God and Moses would refer to the Israelites as "these people," "this people," and "Your people." The Israelites were so corrupt that after a while, God wasn't calling them "My people" anymore. Moses actually asked God once to kill him rather than have to lead "this people" alone (Numbers 11:15).

When it is our time to depart and to be with the Lord, why are most men so reluctant? I believe that the reluctance comes from not wanting to hurt their loved ones who remain and who try so hard to hold on to them. I believe the departing ones suffer on earth to keep their loved ones from suffering their loss, and they stay as long as possible. I believe mothers do this the most because that is their nature, to look after the children. Often, I believe they are ready and even long for their Heavenly mansions and place of rest. What do you hold more dearly on this earth than God and your salvation? Your actions answer for you. Is it time to start letting go, so you can focus on what is really important?

Colossians 3:4 proclaims, *"When Christ, who is our life, shall appear, then shall ye also appear with him in glory."* Is this real to you? Is Christ your LIFE? Is this your reality? Can you HONESTLY say that "Christ"—not your spouse, not your child, not your pastor, neither your job nor family, but CHRIST is your LIFE? Our actual longing and desire should be the same as we sing and preach – to see Jesus.

> *"Therefore we are always confident, knowing that, whilst we are at home in the body, we are absent from the Lord: . . . We are confident, I say, and willing rather to be absent from the body, and to be present with the Lord"* (2 Corinthians 5:6, 8).

Does this mean we should not be happy on this earth? Not at all, *"for I have learned, in whatsoever state I am, therewith to be content"* (Philippians 4:11). The longer the time you have on earth, the more lives you can impact and the more souls you can win for the kingdom. We must be about our Father's business. We must work while it is day, while we are able. One day, we won't be able to work anymore.

Keep in mind that we must not try to put ourselves in the place of Death by taking our own

45

lives. That would be murder, and God has commanded, *"Thou shalt not kill"* (Exodus 20:13; Deuteronomy 5:17; Romans 13:9). Instead, we should live in *patient* waiting for our heavenly bodies as we become all that God has purposed for us in the earth. We should live in love, peace, joy and happiness here, working in God's kingdom.

Simultaneously, we live in joyful anticipation of the moment our work is done and our lives here are over. That is a victorious moment for the child of God. Yes, the hearts of those who remain on earth are saddened because the loved one will no longer be here physically, but for the Believer who transitions, this separation is a victorious moment indeed.

"Now this I say, brethren, that flesh and blood cannot inherit the kingdom of God . . . Death is swallowed up in victory" (1 Corinthians 15:50, 54).

Should we strive for earthly wealth?

What is the Saint's attitude toward earthly possessions?

There are those who have and those who have not. Those who have, do they have because they have worked hard to earn the wealth and thus, deserve it? Not always. The ones who do not have, is it because they have *not* worked hard all their lives, and thus, deserve to be in poverty or to have just enough? Again, not always. Each person's story is unique and worthy of attention. If we cared to bear one another's burden, we would learn much about the plight of our sisters and brothers.

> *"I returned, and saw under the sun, that the race is not to the swift, nor the battle to the strong, neither yet bread to the wise, nor yet riches to men of understanding, nor yet favour to men of skill; but time and chance happeneth to them all"* (Ecclesiastes 9:11).

I stress again. The Scriptures are clear, when we read and listen to what God is telling us, instead of trying so hard to make the words say what we want them to say or what we wish they said. Let us acknowledge that no treasure we have on this earth is really ours. We are not really the ones who have control over wealth. It is in God's power to shut up heaven that it rains no more or to open heaven, and allow the rain. People lose the homes and houses of their dreams all the time. They are called "disasters." People suddenly lose businesses and have all sorts of trouble, or their lives can be required of them, and then, whose riches are they?

> *"But God said unto him, Thou fool, this night thy soul shall be required of thee: then whose shall those things be, which thou hast provided? So is he that layeth up treasure for himself, and is not rich toward God"* (Luke 12:20-21).

> *"If ye then be risen with Christ, seek those things which are above, where Christ sitteth on the right hand of God. Set your affection on things above, not on things on the earth"* (Colossians 3:1-2).

Yes. The Scriptures admonish us to build an inheritance for our seed. *"If you obey God, you will have something to leave your grandchildren. If you don't obey God, those who live right will get what you leave"* (Proverbs 13:22, Contemporary English Version). However, making wealth should not be our primary focus. Our focus must be on obeying God. We must do all the will of God, not just a part.

The blessings that God allows us to obtain or to receive are not to be selfishly kept to ourselves for our gain, but our abundance is also to give to others who have need. How are we using our blessings to help others? How are we using what God has given us to build and advance His Kingdom above our own? Did not Solomon build the temple of God before he built his own house?

The strength, success and value of one's wealth is not in how much we have gained and stored up but in how much we have given to help others and to advance the gospel. Some of the final teachings of Paul include:

"I have shewed you all things, how that so labouring ye ought to support the weak, and to remember the words of the Lord Jesus, how he said, It is more blessed to give than to receive" (Acts 20:35).

Consider also these verses:

"Then He said to them, "Beware, and be on your guard against every form of greed; for not even when one has an abundance does his life consist of his possessions" (Luke 12:15, NASB).

"For all these things do the nations of the world seek after: and your Father knoweth that ye have need of these things. But rather seek ye the kingdom

of God; and all these things shall be added unto you. Fear not, little flock; for it is your Father's good pleasure to give you the kingdom. Sell that ye have, and give alms; provide yourselves bags which wax not old, a treasure in the heavens that faileth not, where no thief approacheth, neither moth corrupteth. For where your treasure is, there will your heart be also" (Luke 12:30-34).

"Go thy way, eat thy bread with joy, and drink thy wine with a merry heart; for God now accepteth thy works. Let thy garments be always white; and let thy head lack no ointment. Live joyfully with the wife whom thou lovest all the days of the life of thy vanity, which he hath given thee under the sun, all the days of thy vanity: for that is thy portion in this life, and in thy labour which thou takest under the sun. Whatsoever thy hand findeth to do, do it with thy might; for there is no work, nor device, nor knowledge, nor wisdom, in the grave, whither thou goest" (Ecclesiastes 9:7-10).

So, should we strive for wealth? What should be our attitude toward earthly possessions? What is the purpose of our life? What is the purpose of death?

Like Christ, we are not born to this world to stay forever. We are sent here with purpose and for a purpose. Throughout life, we must obey God to be in alignment with that purpose, knowing that we shall only pass this way once. Then,

> *"And as it is appointed unto men once to die, but after this the judgment: So Christ was once offered to bear the sins of many; and unto them that look for him shall he appear the second time without sin unto salvation"* (Hebrews 9:27-28).

We live now to live again forever. How will your forever be? Where will you spend your ever after?

Images by Clay L

Dr. Arlene Kearns Dowdy, native of North Carolina, has traveled abundantly and lived abroad. She, now, resides in New Jersey with her beloved husband and childhood sweetheart.

Dr. Dowdy has several other books available on Amazon.com as well as the GLO web page https://www.glotap.org.

Feel free to contact her on Facebook, Twitter or Instagram under her name or Dr. Dowdy Author. You can also subscribe to her You Tube channel that is under Dr. Dowdy Author as well.

Additionally, you may contact her for prayer for healing, encouragement, to discuss this topic further in Bible Study, or

whatever your needs may be. You may also email her at
DrDowdyAuthor@gmail.com.

Other Books by This Author

Tales of Eastwood (2014)
More Tales of Eastwood (2018)
Sacred Secret Seed: A Love Deferred (2019)
For Our Children, Our Future (2018)
There is Purpose in Your Valley (2015)